AF490982
EASY ENGLISH
Christmas
SHORT STORIES
JENNY GOLDMANN

BELLANOVA

MELBOURNE · SOFIA · BERLIN

Christmas Short Stories in Easy English

Get the latest offers and giveaways:
www.bellanovabooks.com/newsletter

Copyright © 2023 by Jenny Goldmann

Imprint: Bellanova Books

Contents

Introduction 4

Christmas Vocabulary 9

The Christmas Exchange 12

Lost and Found in Santa's Workshop 27

The Mysterious Caroler 42

Elf's First Flight 59

The Holiday Mix-up 78

The Lost Reindeer 91

Christmas at the Lighthouse 107

The Magical Snow Globe 125

Molly's Enchanted Christmas Scarf 142

The Christmas Train 158

Introduction

Welcome, dear readers, to "Christmas Short Stories in Easy English"! This book is packed with stories that will take you to snowy towns, cozy homes, and magical winter moments—all while helping you get better at English in a fun way.

Dive into special Christmas tales with characters who discover the joy and magic of the holiday season. Each story is written in English that's a bit simpler but still keeps the charm and warmth of the season. This book is perfect for those who are learning English and also for those who just love heartwarming Christmas stories.

But, there's more! After each story, you'll find some new words, a quiz to see what you remember, and questions to make you think and talk about the story. It's a great way to practice English and chat about the special moments in the tales.

So, readers, get ready. Find a comfy spot, grab a cup of hot cocoa, and dive into the sparkling world of Christmas. Enjoy the stories and let the magic of the season help your English shine!

Happy reading and learning to all!

How to use this book

To get the most out of this book, we recommend the following tips:

DON'T SKIP AHEAD: The stories in this book are arranged in order of increasing difficulty, allowing you to gradually build on your language skills as you progress through the book. This structured approach will help you to better comprehend and absorb the intricacies of the English language. As such, we strongly recommend not skipping any stories, as each one is designed to challenge you slightly more than the one before it.

READ REGULARLY: Make a habit of reading in English on a regular basis. This will help you to build up your vocabulary and grammar skills over time.

TAKE NOTES: As you read, take notes on new words and phrases that you come across. You can also note down sentence structures and grammar rules that you find difficult to understand.

PRACTICE SPEAKING: Use the new vocabulary and grammar that you have learned in the short stories in your conversations with other English speakers. This will help you to internalize the language and improve your fluency.

TEST YOURSELF: Use the quiz at the end of each story to test your knowledge, and use the speaking/writing prompts to challenge yourself even further.

STAY POSITIVE: When you read a book in a new language, you might not know every word. That's okay! Don't worry too much about the words you don't know. Instead, try to understand the story using the words you do know. If you don't know a word, you can write it down and look it up later. Reading is supposed to be fun, so don't worry too much if you don't know every word. Just focus on what you understand and enjoy the story.

JOIN OUR FACEBOOK GROUP:

We understand that learning a new language can be even more effective and fun when done in a community. That's why we've created our special Facebook Group! Here, you can connect with other readers, share your thoughts about the stories, ask questions, and practice your English in a supportive and interactive environment. **Just scan the QR code below:**

Christmas Vocabulary

- **advent *(noun)*:** the period of four weeks before Christmas during which people prepare for the holiday.
- **bauble *(noun)*:** a small, shiny ball or decoration, usually hung on a Christmas tree.
- **carol *(noun)*:** a song sung during the Christmas season.
- **chimney *(noun)*:** a structure through which smoke escapes from a fireplace, often where children believe Santa enters the house.
- **eggnog *(noun)*:** a drink made from milk, cream, sugar, whipped egg whites, and egg yolks, often consumed during the Christmas season.

- **elf** *(noun)*: a small, often mischievous creature who helps Santa make toys.
- **festive** *(adj.)*: reflecting the excitement and celebration related to a festival or party, especially Christmas.
- **garland** *(noun)*: a decorative wreath or chain of flowers, leaves, or ribbons hung in a curve as a decoration.
- **holly** *(noun)*: an evergreen plant with sharp prickly leaves and usually red berries, used especially at Christmas.
- **jingle** *(verb)*: to make a light ringing sound, like the bells on a sleigh.
- **jolly** *(adj.)*: happy and cheerful.
- **mistletoe** *(noun)*: a plant with white berries, traditionally hung during Christmas, under which people are encouraged to kiss.
- **nativity** *(noun)*: the birth of Jesus Christ, often represented in art or in a small model called a 'nativity scene'.
- **noel** *(noun)*: another word for Christmas, especially in songs.

- **ornament** *(noun)*: a decorative object, especially one placed on a Christmas tree.
- **poinsettia** *(noun)*: a red or pink plant used as a Christmas decoration.
- **reindeer** *(noun)*: a type of deer found in cold climates, often associated with pulling Santa's sleigh.
- **sleigh** *(noun)*: a large sled used for traveling over snow, often pulled by animals like reindeer.
- **stocking** *(noun)*: a large sock that children hang up on Christmas Eve, hoping it will be filled with presents by Santa Claus.
- **tidings** *(noun)*: news or information, often heard in the phrase "tidings of comfort and joy" from Christmas carols.
- **twinkle** *(verb)*: to shine with a flickering or sparkling light, like stars or Christmas lights.
- **wreath** *(noun)*: a ring made of flowers, leaves, or other materials that is used as a decoration, especially during Christmas.

The Christmas Exchange

The Global Language College, situated in the heart of New York City, **buzzed** with students from all over the world who were there to learn English. It was early December and with Christmas **approaching**, excitement was in the air.

New York City was a beautiful place to be for Christmas. The **sparkling** lights, decorated stores and the smell of roasting chestnuts made the city feel like something out of a Hollywood Christmas movie.

After a day of exploring the city, the students came together in the large lounge room, where they liked to relax in the evenings. Lisa from Germany **lounged** on the worn-out couch, chatting with Ken from Japan.

"Back home, we have beautiful Christmas markets—they're so much fun," said Lisa.

Ken nodded, smiling. "In Japan, Christmas isn't a traditional holiday. However, it's still a lot of fun. Cities light up, and we often enjoy a special strawberry Christmas cake. Did you know we also like to eat KFC on Christmas Eve?! Weird, I know!"

Their conversation was soon joined by others in the lounge. Maria from Mexico talked about 'Las Posadas', the traditional Mexican **reenactment** of Mary and Joseph's search for somewhere to stay. Pedro from Brazil spoke about attending midnight mass and then feasting, while Anna from Russia shared tales of Grandfather Frost.

While listening to all the conversations, Lisa had a brilliant idea. "Why don't we do a Global Language Christmas gift exchange? Gifts should represent our homes."

Everyone was very excited. They drew names from a hat and started planning their gifts. For days, the college was a hub of activity. Whispers, **giggles**, **sneaky** shopping bags, and late-night crafting were everywhere.

But three days before the exchange, a city-wide **snowstorm** warning was announced.

The weather grew severe, and the roads were blocked. Deliveries were stopped, and public transport was cancelled.

Lisa, the most organized of the group, already had her German gift ready. However, she realized many students who had ordered online or were waiting to buy local New York treats were now in a **bind**.

Ken was amongst the worried students. "The special Japanese treat I ordered for Anna won't arrive now," he said with sadness in his eyes.

Maria sighed, "I was going to the market today to gather the last of what I needed. This storm has ruined my plan!"

Pedro **chimed in**, "Same here. I was buying something from a Brazilian store downtown."

It was clear many students faced challenges due to the snowstorm. Lisa, always the problem solver, called for an emergency meeting in the common room. "We can't control the weather, but we can control our Christmas spirit!"

She suggested a "Creativity Challenge." Using only materials available in the college and their personal items, each student had to craft or create a gift that represented their country. Time limit: 48 hours.

A **flurry** of excitement followed. Ken started folding **origami** creations. Maria, with her artistic skills, began painting beautiful Mexican landscapes on stones she had collected earlier in the year. Pedro wrote a heartfelt poem capturing the **essence** of a Brazilian Christmas.

The next days saw a flurry of activity.

The common room became a temporary workshop filled with laughter, excitement, and the occasional yelp of surprise.

On the evening of the exchange, the air was filled with **anticipation**. Students gathered around the big Christmas tree, gifts in hand. One by one, they presented their handmade, heartfelt gifts. The stories behind each creation made the evening incredibly special.

Ken's origami was a massive success, especially when he **revealed** hidden notes inside. Maria's painted stones, with their **vibrant** colors, were a beautiful representation of her homeland. Pedro's poem, when **recited** out loud, moved many to tears.

By the end, it was clear that while the snowstorm had initially appeared to ruin their Christmas plans, it had pushed everyone to **think outside the box** and provided the gift of creativity and genuine expressions of love.

Lisa ended the evening, "Nature gave us snow, and we responded with love. This has been the best Christmas exchangeever!"

After the exchange, Lisa took a moment to reflect. "While it's been wonderful sharing our traditions and experiencing Christmases from around the world, we're in one of the most iconic places to celebrate Christmas! We should make the most of it."

Anna nodded in agreement, "How about we head to the Rockefeller Center? I've heard they have a magnificent ice skating rink every Christmas, with a giant Christmas tree beside it."

Ken's eyes lit up, "I've never been ice skating before!"

Maria laughed, "Me neither! This will be fun."

Thankfully, by the time the gift exchange had ended, the snowstorm had passed, leaving behind a beautiful blanket of white. The city looked even more magical under its fresh coat of snow.

With their energy high, the group decided to head out. They **bundled up** in their warmest clothes and headed to the Rockefeller Center. The iconic ice rink shimmered under the night sky, the massive Christmas tree beside it, **illuminated** with thousands of twinkling lights.

One by one, the students from the Global Language College put on their ice skates. For many, it was their first time. They held onto each other, laughing and tumbling.

As they skated in the shadow of the beautiful tree, with the city lights shining off the snow-covered buildings, they felt the full magic of a New York City Christmas. The evening was filled with joy, laughter, and a few clumsy falls, but it only added to their collection of wonderful memories.

Back in the college, as they sat **nursing** their sore feet and sipping on hot cocoa, they all agreed: The unexpected problem of the snowstorm, the creativity challenge, and the ice-skating adventure had made it a Christmas they would never forget.

New Words

- **buzz *(verb)*:** make a low, continuous humming sound.
- **approach *(verb)*:** come near or nearer to.
- **sparkle *(verb)*:** shine brightly with flashes of light.
- **lounge *(verb)*:** sit or stand in a relaxed way.
- **reenactment *(noun)*:** the act of performing a role in an event that occurred at an earlier time.
- **giggle *(verb)*:** laugh lightly in a nervous or silly way.
- **sneaky *(adj.)*:** acting in a secretive or deceitful manner; done in a way to avoid notice or attention.
- **snowstorm *(noun)*:** a heavy fall of snow, especially with a high wind.
- **bind *(noun)*:** a problematic situation.
- **chime in *(phrasal verb)*:** to interject or join a conversation, often to express an opinion or add a comment.

- **flurry *(noun)*:** a sudden burst or commotion, often related to emotions or activities; in the story, it refers to a surge of excitement.
- **origami *(noun)*:** the traditional Japanese art of folding paper into decorative shapes and figures.
- **essence *(noun)*:** the most important ingredient; the crucial element.
- **anticipate *(verb)*:** expect or predict something.
- **reveal *(verb)*:** make previously unknown information known.
- **vibrant *(adj.)*:** bright and striking.
- **recite *(verb)*:** repeat aloud from memory.
- **think outside the box *(phrase)*:** to think creatively and unconventionally.
- **bundle up *(verb)*:** dress in warm clothing.
- **shimmer *(verb)*:** shine with a soft tremulous light.
- **illuminate *(verb)*:** light up.
- **nurse *(verb)*:** to take care of or tend to someone, or oneself.

1. Where is the Global Language College located?
- a) Tokyo
- b) Sydney
- c) New York City
- d) Moscow

2. What was special about Christmas in Germany, as mentioned by Lisa?
- a) It snows a lot.
- b) It's in the winter.
- c) They eat special cakes.
- d) They have beautiful Christmas markets.

3. What is a tradition in Japan during Christmas as shared by Ken?

    a) Having a big family dinner.

    b) Eating KFC on Christmas Eve.

    c) Exchanging gifts with neighbors.

    d) Going to the beach.

4. Why did the students initially face challenges with the gift exchange?

    a) They forgot about it.

    b) There was a city-wide snowstorm.

    c) The college banned gift exchanges.

    d) They didn't like each other's ideas.

5. What was Lisa's solution to the snowstorm problem?

    a) To cancel the gift exchange.

    b) To ask the college for help.

    c) A "Creativity Challenge" using only materials available in the college.

    d) To buy gifts from a nearby store.

Discussion

1. Have you ever faced a challenging situation during a holiday or celebration? How did you overcome it?

2. Imagine you were part of the Global Language College's gift exchange. What kind of gift would you create to represent your country or culture?

3. If you could spend Christmas in any city in the world, where would it be and why?

ANSWERS:

1. c) New York City
2. d) They have beautiful Christmas markets.
3. b) Eating KFC on Christmas Eve.
4. b) There was a city-wide snowstorm.
5. c) A "Creativity Challenge" using only materials available in the college.

Lost and Found in Santa's Workshop

The **North Pole** was covered in soft snow, and the stars shone brightly in the sky. Not far away, reindeer made soft sounds, and their bells jingled. In the middle of this snowy place was Santa's **workshop**. It was a wooden building with lights shining from its windows. From inside, you could hear the happy sounds of elves working and singing. This was where all the Christmas toys were made.

The workshop was buzzing with energy. Elves were everywhere, preparing for the most exciting night of the year. Among the piles of toys was Timmy, a small **tin soldier**.

He had been painted perfectly. His uniform was shiny and bright, and he wore a small **rifle** by his side.

Timmy had heard that he was going to a new home in Australia, and he was very excited to be there. It was far too cold for him in the North Pole.

However, the workshop was as busy as ever, and as the elves sorted the toys into large **sacks** for delivery, a young elf named Ella accidentally knocked Timmy off the table. There was so much noise in the workshop that Ella didn't hear him fall. Timmy landed in a corner behind a tall stack of toy boxes.

"Oh no!" gasped Timmy, trying to get up. "I need to be in Jamie's sack. He's been waiting for me."

The workshop was huge. It was a **maze** of toys, gifts, and wrapping paper. "How will I ever find my way back?" he thought. "This will take forever!"

Suddenly, he heard a soft voice. "Lost, are you?" It was Penny, a cute **ragdoll** with **yarn** for hair and **rosy cheeks**. "I've been here for a long time. I got lost during last year's sorting and Christmas was over before I could find my way back. But don't worry, I now know this place **like the back of my hand**! Together we can find your sack."

Timmy was relieved to meet such a friendly toy. He smiled as he agreed to join Penny on a mission to find his sack.

With Penny leading the way, they navigated through the workshop. But it wasn't straightforward. They encountered a group of **mischievous wind-up mice** playing **pranks**. "You can't pass unless you beat us in a race," **squeaked** the leader.

The race wasn't simple. It was through a maze of toy mountains and tiny tunnels, with toy cars and spinning tops as obstacles. Timmy worried about the challenge, but he was brave. "Alright, we'll race. Penny, jump on my back."

Penny held on tight. As the race began, the mice ran ahead, their tiny feet moving fast. Timmy, with Penny cheering for him, focused hard. He dodged the spinning tops and climbed over the toy mountains. At the last tunnel, with a final push, Timmy sped past the mice and reached the finish line.

"Hooray!" cheered Penny. "We did it together!"

The duo continued their journey. They climbed mountains of **stuffed bears** and trekked through valleys of **board games**. Along the way, they met Oliver, a toy **owl** with knowledge about every corner of the workshop.

"I've seen Jamie's sack!" **hooted** Oliver.

"But it's on the other side, near the reindeer stables."

Feeling hopeful, the trio moved forward, but another challenge was waiting for them. A river of shiny ribbons blocked their path. Timmy was puzzled. "How do we cross this?"

Penny had an idea. She began **braiding** the **ribbons**, creating a strong bridge. "Hurry!" she exclaimed. "Time is running out."

Crossing the ribbon bridge, they could see the reindeer stables and, not too far away, Jamie's sack. But suddenly, they were stopped by a group of **nutcracker** soldiers. "Stop! No one passes without the password."

Timmy stepped forward, **saluting** them. "Fellow soldiers, I must reach that sack for Christmas. Please let us pass."

The chief nutcracker looked sternly at Timmy, then broke into a smile. "No password needed for a brother. Go on."

Finally, they reached the sack. Timmy, with Penny's and Oliver's help, climbed in. "I made it! Thank you both," he whispered, feeling grateful.

Penny smiled, "It was quite an adventure, wasn't it?"

Oliver winked, "Every toy deserves a home."

As Christmas day **dawned** and children worldwide found their presents, Jamie unwrapped Timmy, his eyes shining with joy. Timmy was very much loved and even got to visit the beach and see a **kangaroo**.

Back in the workshop, Penny was picked up by Ella, who had noticed her.

"Oh, here you are!" she exclaimed. "You're just perfect for little Lucy."

As for Oliver, he became the official guide for lost toys, ensuring every toy found its rightful place.

The **legend** of Timmy's adventurous night became a favorite story among the elves, reminding them of the spirit of teamwork, adventure, and the **magic** of Christmas.

New Words

- **North Pole *(noun)*:** the point in the northern hemisphere where the Earth's axis of rotation meets its surface.
- **workshop *(noun)*:** a place where things are made or repaired; in this story, it's where toys are made.
- **tin soldier *(noun)*:** a small toy made of metal and shaped like a soldier.
- **rifle *(noun)*:** a type of gun, here referring to the toy version.
- **sack *(noun)*:** a bag made of a thick paper or fabric.
- **maze *(noun)*:** a complex network of paths or passages.
- **ragdoll *(noun)*:** a soft toy doll made from cloth.
- **yarn *(noun)*:** a long, thin strand of cotton or other fibers used in sewing or weaving.

- **rosy cheeks** *(noun phrase)*: pink-colored cheeks, often indicating health or warmth.
- **like the back of my hand** *(phrase)*: to know something very well or be very familiar with it.
- **mischievous** *(adj.)*: playful in a naughty or teasing way.
- **wind-up mouse** *(noun phrase)*: a toy mouse that moves when wound up by a key or knob.
- **prank** *(noun)*: playful trick or joke.
- **squeak** *(verb)*: to make a short, high-pitched sound.
- **stuffed bear** *(noun phrase)*: toy bears filled with soft material.
- **board game** *(noun phrase)*: a game that is played on a flat surface with pieces, cards, dice, etc.
- **owl** *(noun)*: a bird known for its large eyes and nighttime hunting.

- **hoot** *(verb)*: the sound that owls make.
- **ribbon** *(noun)*: narrow strip of fabric, often used for tying or decoration.
- **braid** *(verb)*: intertwining three or more strands of flexible material like hair or fabric.
- **nutcracker** *(noun)*: a tool to crack nuts; here, it refers to toy soldiers that resemble these tools.
- **salute** *(verb)*: a gesture of respect, especially in the military, by raising one's hand to the forehead.
- **kangaroo** *(noun)*: a large marsupial from Australia known for hopping on its hind legs.
- **legend** *(noun)*: a story from the past that's believed by many but cannot be proved to be true.
- **magic** *(noun)*: the power to make impossible things happen by saying special words or performing special actions.

Test yourself

1. Where did Timmy, the tin soldier, land after being knocked off the table?

    a) In Jamie's sack.

    b) On top of a mountain of stuffed bears.

    c) In a corner behind a tall stack of toy boxes.

    d) Near the group of mischievous wind-up mice.

2. Who did Timmy first meet when he realized he was lost?

    a) Oliver, the knowledgeable owl.

    b) The chief nutcracker.

    c) The leader of the wind-up mice.

    d) Penny, the ragdoll.

3. What challenge did the wind-up mice present to Timmy and Penny?

a) They asked for the password to pass.

b) They challenged them to a race.

c) They hid Jamie's sack.

4. What obstacle did Timmy, Penny, and Oliver face near the reindeer stables?

a) A river of shiny ribbons.

b) A maze of toy mountains and tunnels.

c) A group of playful elves.

5. Who became the official guide for lost toys in Santa's workshop?

a) Timmy, the tin soldier.

b) Penny, the ragdoll.

c) Oliver, the toy owl.

Discussion

1. Why is teamwork important during tough times? Can you give a personal example of when teamwork helped you?

2. How did Timmy's determination help him? Why is being determined important to reach goals? Talk about a time you had to be determined.

3. At the end of the story, each toy has a place. Why is finding where we belong important? What does "belonging" mean to you?

1. c) In a corner behind a tall stack of toy boxes.
2. d) Penny, the ragdoll.
3. b) They challenged them to a race.
4. a) A river of shiny ribbons.
5. c) Oliver, the toy owl.

The Mysterious Caroler

Evergreen Street seemed like the **picture-perfect** American neighborhood. It had charming homes with white **picket fences** and neighbors would say 'good morning!' to everyone they passed. But beneath its **seemingly** normal **exterior**, this friendly street held a **mysterious** secret.

When winter came and snow covered the ground, something special happened.

Every evening, families would hear someone singing outside. It was a beautiful voice that sang Christmas songs.

"Silent night, holy night..."

The **notes** were pure, tender, and held a **haunting** beauty. Residents would **peek** from behind curtains, trying to glimpse the singer, but all they saw was a **shadowy** figure, hidden by the falling snow, disappearing as mysteriously as they had come.

Nora, a **retired** schoolteacher who had lived on Evergreen Street for decades, was particularly **intrigued** and wanted to find out who the mysterious caroler was.

After one particularly **enchanting rendition** of "Away in a Manger", Nora found herself sitting by her **fireplace**, sipping on a cup of tea, lost in memories. Her late husband, Robert, had always loved carolers. Every Christmas, they'd sit by their window, a blanket wrapped around them, listening to the children from the neighborhood sing.

Robert would **hum** along, his deep voice harmonizing perfectly with the young ones outside. Nora remembered how, one year, he had surprised her by joining the kids, his **baritone** voice adding a new layer of beauty to the song. Those memories were a

bittersweet reminder of past Christmases.

One morning, she shared these memories with her neighbor Phil as they were talking over the fence in her garden. "You know, Phil," Nora began, her voice soft, "every time I hear that caroler, I feel like Robert's right here with me, humming along."

Phil looked at Nora with understanding in his eyes. "That's why you want to find out who it is, isn't it, Mrs. Nora?"

Nora nodded. "Yes. In a way, that voice, it's like a gift. A connection to happier times. I just want to thank them."

Phil nodded, "I've tried looking for them too, Mrs. Nora. It's like they appear and disappear with the snow."

Suddenly, Phil's eyes lit up with excitement.

"What if we try to capture them on camera? I have some equipment we could set up."

Nora thought this was an amazing idea. So, Phil, with his **tech-savviness**, set up cameras at various points on the street, hoping to capture the mysterious caroler on film. However, each time they watched the footage, the singer avoided them. Either the cameras **malfunctioned**, or the figure was just **out of frame**, leaving them with more questions than answers.

Frustrated, Nora said, "It's like they know we are trying to find them!"

Phil agreed, "It's very odd. The camera should have caught something."

One evening, Nora had an idea. "Why don't we organize a neighborhood caroling evening? We could invite everyone. Maybe our mysterious caroler will join, and we can finally meet them.”

Phil smiled, “That's a brilliant idea, Mrs. Nora!”

Word spread and the idea was **met with enthusiasm**. The residents of Evergreen Street gathered at Nora's house, **sipping hot cocoa** and practicing carols.

As they began moving from house to house, Nora and Phil kept an eye out for any new faces, anyone who might be their caroler. Yet, everyone seemed familiar.

As the evening **wore on**, disappointment began to cloud the festive spirit. It seemed the mysterious caroler wouldn't reveal themselves.

But as the group approached the last house,

a soft voice rose above the rest, singing a rendition of "O Holy Night." The voice was **unmistakably** that of the mysterious caroler.

The crowd fell silent, turning to see a middle-aged woman, tears in her eyes, lost in the melody. It was Mrs. Henderson, the quiet **widow** from the end of the street.

As the last note lingered in the cold air, she looked around, realizing all eyes were on her. "I... I didn't think anyone noticed," she began, her voice trembling. "It's just... these carols, they were my late husband's favorites. Every Christmas, we used to sing them together. After he passed away, singing them became a way for me to feel close to him, to remember the beautiful moments we shared."

Nora approached Mrs. Henderson, **enveloping** her in a warm hug. "Why didn't you tell me? Your voice brought comfort to all of us. We just wanted to know the angel behind it."

Mrs. Henderson smiled through her tears. "Every note, every word, it's like I'm singing with him again."

Nora nodded, understandingly. "I felt the same way with my Robert. Those carols, they're not just songs, they're memories. Memories of times when our loved ones were right beside us."

Mrs. Henderson took Nora's hands in hers, "It's amazing, isn't it? How a simple melody can **evoke** such powerful emotions."

The two women shared a quiet moment, connected by their shared grief and the memories that carols brought back.

Phil, moved by the connection, added, "Why

don't you both start a caroling group? In honor of your husbands. It could be a way to keep their memory alive and to bring joy to others."

Nora's eyes lit up. "That's a wonderful idea, Phil! What do you think, Mrs. Henderson?"

Mrs. Henderson nodded enthusiastically, "I think it's a beautiful way to remember them. And to share the love and warmth of carols with everyone."

The following week, Nora and Mrs. Henderson put up **notices** around Evergreen Street, inviting residents to join their new caroling group, **aptly named** "Echoes of the Past." The group quickly grew, as many were drawn to the idea of singing in memory of loved ones and for the sheer joy of community bonding.

The first caroling event hosted by "Echoes of the Past" was a heartwarming success, with Nora and Mrs. Henderson leading the group, their voices ringing out in **harmony**, filled with love, memories, and the spirit of the season.

And so, as years passed, the tradition continued, and the voices of "Echoes of the Past" became a tradition of Evergreen Street's winter nights. The mysterious caroler wasn't so mysterious anymore, but the magic she brought that first night would be remembered forever.

New Words

- **picture-perfect *(adj.)*:** ideal or flawless, something that looks as good as a well-taken photograph.
- **picket fences *(noun)*:** a type of fence that's often seen as typical of an idyllic suburban or rural house in the U.S.
- **seemingly *(adverb)*:** based on appearance; not necessarily in reality.
- **exterior *(noun)*:** the outer surface or appearance of something.
- **mysterious *(adj.)*:** something hard to explain or understand.
- **caroler *(noun)*:** a person who sings Christmas carols.
- **notes *(noun)*:** individual tones of music.
- **haunting *(adj.)*:** something so beautiful it's unforgettable.

- **peek *(verb)*:** to look quickly or sneakily.
- **shadowy *(adj.)*:** not clearly visible or defined.
- **figure *(noun)*:** a person or shape.
- **retired *(adj.)*:** describing someone who used to work but no longer does.
- **intrigued *(adj.)*:** very interested.
- **rendition *(noun)*:** a particular version or interpretation, in this case of a song.
- **enchanting *(adj.)*:** captivating or charming.
- **fireplace *(noun)*:** a place in a room where you can make a fire.
- **hum *(verb)*:** to sing a tune with closed lips.
- **baritone *(noun)*:** a deep male singing voice.
- **bittersweet *(adj.)*:** a mix of happiness and sadness.
- **tech-savviness *(noun)*:** knowledge about modern technology.
- **malfunctioned *(verb)*:** broke down or failed to work.

- **out of frame** *(adjective phrase)*: not visible in the recorded video or picture.
- **met with enthusiasm** *(verb phrase)*: received with excitement.
- **sip** *(verb)*: drinking in small amounts.
- **hot cocoa** *(noun)*: a warm drink made from cocoa powder.
- **wear on (past tense: wore on)** *(verb phrase)*: continued over time.
- **unmistakably** *(adverb)*: clearly, without any doubt.
- **widow** *(noun)*: a woman whose husband has died.
- **envelope** *(verb)*: wrapping or surrounding completely.
- **evoke** *(verb)*: to bring to mind or recollect a feeling, memory, or image.
- **notices** *(noun)*: announcements or information.
- **aptly named** *(adjective phrase)*: suitably named.

1. What was special about Evergreen Street during winter?

      a) It hosted a Christmas market.

      b) Families would hear someone singing outside.

      c) They had a winter carnival every year.

2. Why was Nora particularly interested in the mysterious caroler?

      a) She thought the caroler might be a relative.

      b) The caroler reminded her of her late husband, Robert.

      c) She wanted to invite the caroler to her Christmas party.

3. What was Phil's idea to find out the identity of the mysterious caroler?

    a) To invite the caroler to a party.

    b) To follow the caroler's tracks in the snow.

    c) To set up cameras.

4. Who turned out to be the mysterious caroler?

    a) A young girl from another street.

    b) Nora's distant relative.

    c) Mrs. Henderson, the widow from the end of the street.

5. What did Nora and Mrs. Henderson decide to do in memory of their late husbands?

    a) They decided to write a book.

    b) They chose to plant trees in their memory.

    c) They started a caroling group named "Echoes of the Past."

Discussion

1. What is your neighborhood like? Do people greet each other on the streets?

2. What do you think about Christmas carols? Do you have a favorite?

3. Is there a special song that reminds you of a happy memory or a special person in your life? What is it and why?

4. Have you ever experienced something mysterious in your neighborhood, like the unknown caroler on Evergreen Street? What was it?

ANSWERS

1. b) Families would hear someone singing outside.
2. b) The caroler reminded her of her late husband, Robert.
3. c) To set up cameras.
4. c) Mrs. Henderson, the widow from the end of the street.
5. c) They started a caroling group named "Echoes of the Past."

Elf's First Flight

In the heart of the North Pole, where snow never stopped falling, Santa's village bustled with excitement. Christmas was around the corner, and every elf was working **tirelessly**. But this year was particularly special for one young elf named Eddy.

Eddy was in the workshop, **diligently** painting toy trains alongside his best friend, Lila. They'd been inseparable since they were young elves, always sharing stories and dreams. Today, Eddy seemed more excited than usual, barely focusing on his painting.

Noticing his distraction, Lila asked, "Something on your mind, Eddy?"

Eddy looked up, his eyes gleaming with excitement. "Lila, I've got some incredible news!"

"Oh? What's that?" Lila responded, her brush pausing mid-stroke.

"Santa's chosen me to **accompany** him on his Christmas Eve **journey**!" Eddy **beamed**.

Lila's eyes widened. "Wow! But aren't you nervous?"

Eddy nodded, "A bit. I've never been beyond the North Pole. What's the world like out there?"

Lila giggled, "Well, I haven't been either! But I hear there are places without snow!"

Eddy **gasped**. "No snow? Impossible!"

Days passed, and soon it was Christmas Eve. Santa, in his big red suit, approached Eddy. "Ready for our big journey?" he said.

Eddy, wearing a new green outfit with bright red shoes, nodded **eagerly**. But inside, he was very nervous.

They hopped onto the magical sleigh, with reindeer at the front and bells jingling. With a loud "Ho, ho, ho!" from Santa and a flick of the **reins**, they were **airborne**.

As they **soared** over the North Pole, Eddy looked down. The snowy village looked tiny. "It's so… different from up here," he whispered.

Santa chuckled, "Wait until you see the rest of the world!"

Their first stop was a city filled with towering buildings with lights shining like stars. Eddy gasped, "What are those, Santa?"

"Skyscrapers," Santa replied. "Quite a **contrast** from our little wooden huts, right?"

Eddy nodded in amazement.

In one house, they went down the **chimney**, and Eddy was struck by the warmth. The stockings were hung, and cookies and milk lay on a table.

Eddy sniffed, "It smells... different."

Santa smiled, "Every home has its own unique scent. That's **gingerbread**."

They left gifts, ate cookies, and were soon back in the chilly air. The journey took them over deserts, forests, mountains, and seas. Each time, Eddy had a million questions, and Santa answered patiently.

"Why is that water so big?" Eddy wondered as they flew over an ocean.

"That's the Pacific Ocean," Santa explained. "Much bigger than our little Arctic Ocean."

They visited homes of all sorts: big **mansions**, cozy **cottages**, apartments in tall buildings, and even tents in deserts.

In a small village, they entered a home where children had left carrots for the reindeer and letters for Santa with their hopes and wishes. Eddy picked up a letter and read, *"Dear Santa, we don't need toys. Just happiness for our family."*

Eddy looked up, eyes moist, "They don't want toys?"

Santa nodded, "Sometimes, the simplest wishes are the most powerful."

After reading the letter, Santa paused, deep in thought. He then reached into his bag and pulled out a small, beautifully woven basket filled with seeds.

"Eddy," he whispered, "these are magical seeds. When planted, they'll bring crops throughout the year, no matter the weather. It'll ensure the family has food, and they can even sell the extras at the market. It'll ease some **burdens** and bring them closer together." Eddy nodded, understanding the amazing impact such a gift could have.

They carried on their journey, and the night was full of wonders for Eddy. In one country, he saw children playing with **firecrackers**. In another, families were singing carols outside homes. He even saw a giant tree in a square with thousands of lights!

But the biggest surprise was on a **tropical** island. They landed on soft sand, and Eddy stepped out. "What is this? It's so warm and... **ticklish**!"

Santa laughed, "That's sand! And this warm place is called a beach."

Eddy danced around, feeling the sand between his toes. "This is fun!"

As they were about to head to their next destination, Santa's sleigh suddenly **jolted**. Eddy, who was lost in the beauty of Earth, was caught **off guard**.

"Whoa! What was that?" Eddy exclaimed.

Santa, looking a bit concerned, replied, "Seems like one of the magical sleigh bells has come loose. Without it, our sleigh might lose its magic!"

Eddy gulped, realizing the **gravity** of the situation. "Is there anything we can do?"

Santa thought for a moment. "We need to replace it with something equally magical to continue our journey. Think, Eddy, think!"

Eddy tried to remember the places they had been to. Then, an idea struck him. "The letters! The children's letters to you, filled with wishes and hopes. Can't we use one of them?"

Santa's face lit up. "Brilliant, Eddy! The pure emotions and innocent wishes in those letters indeed hold a special kind of magic."

They quickly pulled out a heartfelt letter from the sleigh, tied it where the sleigh bell used to be, and soon, the sleigh was flying once again, sprinkling joyous magic all over the world.

As dawn approached, they had one last stop: an **orphanage** nestled in a quiet town. While Santa and Eddy were busy placing gifts, a soft tug pulled at Eddy's shirt. He turned to find a little girl, her big, curious eyes twinkling in the dim light.

"Are you an elf?" she whispered, a hint of wonder in her voice.

Eddy knelt down to her level, offering a gentle smile. "Indeed, I am! My name's Eddy. You should be tucked away in bed, shouldn't you?"

She offered a **sheepish grin**, "I know, but I was just too excited. I'm Lucy. Thank you for all the gifts—they mean a lot to us all."

Eddy enveloped her in a warm embrace, "Merry Christmas, Lucy."

Pulling back slightly and placing a finger on his lips, he added with a playful wink, "And remember, our meeting is our little secret. Deal?"

Lucy giggled, nodding her head, "Deal!"

Soon, they were back in the sleigh, heading home. The North Pole appeared on the horizon, its icy landscape welcoming them.

As they landed, Lila rushed to Eddy. "How was it?"

Eddy's eyes sparkled, "Incredible! The world's so big, so **diverse**. But everywhere, the spirit of Christmas is the same."

Santa, overhearing, added, "And every year, it's the joy in the eyes of young elves like you and children around the world that makes this journey worth it."

Eddy nodded, gratitude and wonder filling his heart. He had seen the world beyond the North Pole and had come back with stories that would last a lifetime.

The following year, Eddy eagerly joined Santa once more on his Christmas Eve journey. As they flew over the familiar landscapes, Santa drove the sleigh towards the small village where they'd delivered the magical seeds. To their delight, they saw a busy farm, its produce feeding not just the family but the entire village. They could hear laughter coming from their homes and their happiness was clear.

And as they later approached the orphanage, a familiar face peered out of a window. It was Lucy, her eyes gleaming brighter than ever, waving enthusiastically.

For Eddy, seeing the real impact of their gifts was the best gift of all.

New words

- **tirelessly *(adverb)*:** without getting tired; continuously.
- **diligently *(adverb)*:** in a careful and persistent manner, showing effort and dedication.
- **accompany *(verb)*:** to go with someone.
- **journey *(noun)*:** a trip or voyage.
- **beam *(verb)*:** smile broadly with happiness.
- **gasp *(verb)*:** take a sudden, short breath, usually in surprise.
- **eagerly *(adverb)*:** with excitement and enthusiasm.
- **reins *(noun)*:** the straps used to control and guide animals like horses or reindeer.
- **airborne *(adj.)*:** up in the air; flying.
- **soar *(verb)*:** fly up high in the sky.

- **skyscrapers** *(noun)*: very tall buildings found in cities.
- **contrast** *(noun)*: being strikingly different from something else.
- **chimney** *(noun)*: a vertical channel in a building through which smoke and gases are carried up to the air.
- **gingerbread** *(noun)*: a sweet, spicy cake or cookie.
- **mansion** *(noun)*: large and impressive house.
- **cottage** *(noun)*: small and simple houses, typically in the countryside.
- **burden** *(noun)*: a heavy load, responsibility, or duty that one must bear or carry; something weighing one down emotionally or mentally.
- **firecrackers** *(noun)*: small fireworks that make a loud noise when they explode.

- **tropical** *(adj.)*: relating to the regions of the Earth near the equator which are very warm.
- **ticklish** *(adj.)*: sensitive to being tickled; easily tickled.
- **jolt** *(verb)*: move suddenly and roughly.
- **off guard** *(adj.)*: unprepared or surprised.
- **gravity** *(noun)*: importance or seriousness of a situation.
- **orphanage** *(noun)*: a home for children without parents.
- **sheepish grin** *(noun)*: a shy or embarrassed smile, often displayed when someone knows they've done something wrong or awkward.
- **diverse** *(adj.)*: varied or different from one another.

Test yourself

1. Why was the year particularly special for Eddy?
>a) He built the largest toy train.
>b) He was chosen to lead the other elves.
>c) He was chosen to accompany Santa on his Christmas Eve journey.

2. What was Eddy's reaction when Lila mentioned places without snow?
>a) He didn't believe such places existed.
>b) He wanted to build snowmen there.
>c) He was indifferent.

3. What are "skyscrapers"?

> a) Houses in the village.
>
> b) Tall trees in the forest.
>
> c) Very tall buildings found in cities.

4. What problem did Santa and Eddy encounter during their journey?

> a) The reindeer got tired.
>
> b) One of the magical sleigh bells came loose.
>
> c) They ran out of gifts.

5. How did they fix the problem with the sleigh bell?

> a) They used a spare bell.
>
> b) They tied a child's toy in its place.
>
> c) They used a child's heartfelt letter.

Discussion

1. Where would you most like to travel in the world and why?

2. How do you celebrate the holiday season in your family or community?

3. Have there been times when you've wished for something intangible, like happiness or love, rather than a physical gift? Share an experience or thought on this.

4. Have you ever experienced something that made you feel like Eddy did when he first saw skyscrapers or the beach? Describe that moment.

ANSWERS

1. c) He was chosen to accompany Santa on his Christmas Eve journey.
2. a) He didn't believe such places existed.
3. c) Very tall buildings found in cities.
4. b) One of the magical sleigh bells came loose.
5. c) They used a child's heartfelt letter.

The Holiday Mix-up

It was a cold winter day at Pine Valley Christmas Tree Farm. **Snowflakes** fell slowly from the sky, covering the ground in white. Everywhere you looked, there were tall green trees ready for Christmas. Mr. Hanson, the owner of the farm, was busy helping families. He loved this time of year and enjoyed seeing happy faces as people picked their favorite tree.

At Pine Valley, families walked around with big smiles. They looked at all the trees, trying to find the best one for their home. Mr. Hanson chatted with parents and played with the children.

Lily Thompson, with her bright eyes and rosy

cheeks, eagerly ran between the **rows** of trees. Suddenly, she tugged at her mom's coat. "Look, Mom! This one's just right!" She pointed at a **medium-sized** tree with thick branches and a lovely shape.

Mrs. Thompson bent down to her daughter, her breath visible in the chilly air. "You like this one, sweetie?"

Lily's eyes sparkled with excitement. "Yes! It's perfect, just like the one in our Christmas storybook."

Not far away, the Davis family was having a **discussion** of their own.

Ben, being a bit taller than his **peers**, had his sights set on one of the **grandest** trees in the lot. "Dad, how about this one?" he asked, pointing upwards.

Mr. Davis chuckled, "It's a bit tall, don't you think?"

Ben grinned, "But imagine all the lights and stars we could put on it!"

Both families, sure of their choices, approached Mr. Hanson to make their purchases, unaware of the mix-up that was soon to **unfold**.

The next day, after the families had set up their trees, Lily walked into her living room and couldn't believe her eyes. "Mom, this isn't our tree!" she exclaimed. The tree in front of her was much taller than the one they had picked out, and it was decorated with **unfamiliar** ornaments.

"What do you mean?" said her mom, **puzzled**. "We got it from Mr. Hanson's Christmas tree farm, just like every year."

Meanwhile, across town, a similar scene was unfolding in the Davis family home.

"Dad, our tree has **shrunk**!" shouted Ben, pointing at the modest tree that now stood in their living room.

Mr. Davis scratched his head. "I picked it up from Mr. Hanson's. There must be some mistake."

Back at the Thompsons, Lily was examining the ornaments on the tree. "Look, Mom, this isn't our star." She pointed at a beautifully **crafted** wooden star. "And who are these people?" She showed her mom a photo ornament of a family she didn't recognize.

Mrs. Thompson had a **sinking feeling**. "Oh dear, we must have taken the Davis family's tree!"

At the same moment, Ben was showing his dad a **handmade** ornament that read "Lily's First Christmas".

"We've got the Thompson's tree, Dad!"

Both families quickly realized the mix-up. Mrs. Thompson called Mrs. Davis.

"Hello, Mrs. Davis? I think we have your tree," Mrs. Thompson said with a laugh.

"Oh! We were just about to call you! We have yours," Mrs. Davis replied, chuckling. "How about we meet tomorrow and exchange our trees?"

The next day, at Pine Valley Christmas tree farm, the two families gathered. As they swapped trees and shared Christmas stories, the atmosphere was full of laughter and **camaraderie**.

Then, Lily had an idea. "Let's swap one ornament each as a memory of this day!"

Everyone nodded in agreement and Lily held up a toy soldier ornament. "This was my grandfather's," she explained. "It's very old and very special."

Ben smiled, handing over a glass angel. "This was on my mom's first Christmas tree when she was a baby."

As they exchanged ornaments and stories, the two families felt a special connection. What started as a mix-up became an afternoon of shared memories and new friendships.

Finally, the trees were back with their **rightful owners**, each with a new special ornament as a **keepsake** of this unique Christmas mix-up.

"Every year, when we put up this ornament," Mrs. Thompson said, holding the glass angel, "we'll remember this day and the lovely Davis family."

Mrs. Davis, holding the toy soldier, replied, "And we'll always have a piece of the Thompsons with us. Merry Christmas!"

From that year on, not only did the two families **double-check** their trees, but they also started a new tradition. Every Christmas, the Thompsons and the Davis family would meet and exchange one special ornament, celebrating the unexpected friendship that came from a holiday mix-up.

New words

- **mix-up *(noun)*:** a confusion or mistake that results from misunderstood or mistaken intentions or actions.
- **snowflake *(noun)*:** small, delicate piece of frozen water that falls from the sky when it snows.
- **row *(noun)*:** line of things arranged side by side.
- **tug *(verb)*:** pull sharply.
- **medium-sized *(adj.)*:** not too big and not too small; of average size.
- **discussion *(noun)*:** a talk or conversation about a specific topic.
- **peer *(noun)*:** people who are of the same age, status, or ability as others.
- **grand *(adj.)*:** impressive and/or large.
- **unfold *(verb)*:** to happen or develop.

- **ornament** *(noun)*: decorative object, often hung on a Christmas tree.
- **puzzle** *(verb; to be puzzled)*: confuse or make uncertain.
- **unfamiliar** *(adj.)*: not known or recognized.
- **shrink** *(verb)*: become smaller in size.
- **craft** *(verb)*: make with skill and care.
- **sinking feeling** *(noun phrase)*: a feeling of disappointment or despair.
- **handmade** *(adj.)*: made by hand, not by machine.
- **camaraderie** *(noun)*: mutual trust and friendship among people who spend a lot of time together.
- **keepsake** *(noun)*: a small item kept in memory of the person who gave it or the event at which it was received.
- **rightful owner** *(noun phrase)*: the correct or legitimate owner of something.
- **double-check** *(verb)*: check again to make sure something is correct or in order.

Test yourself

1. Where did the two families buy their Christmas trees from?

    a) The supermarket
    b) Pine Valley Christmas Tree Farm
    c) A neighbor's backyard

2. How did Lily first realize there was a mix-up?

    a) The tree was taller than the one
       they picked.
    b) She found a letter under the tree.
    c) The tree was a different color.
    d) Mr. Hanson called to tell her.

3. What did Ben say about his family's tree when he saw it at home?

      a) "Our tree has shrunk!"

      b) "Our tree is too big!"

      c) "Our tree looks different."

4. What made the Thompsons realize that they had taken the wrong tree?

      a) They found a toy soldier ornament.

      b) The tree smelled differently.

      c) They saw a photo ornament of a family they didn't recognize.

5. After the mix-up, what new tradition did the Thompsons and the Davis family start?

      a) They bought trees together.

      b) They exchanged Christmas gifts every year.

      c) They would meet and exchange one special ornament every Christmas.

Discussion

1. Do you prefer real or artificial Christmas trees? Why?

2. Can you think of an unexpected event in your life that led to something positive?

3. Do you have a sentimal item that holds memories for you?

ANSWERS

1. b) Pine Valley Christmas Tree Farm.
2. a) The tree was taller than the one they picked.
3. a) "Our tree has shrunk!"
4. c) They saw a photo ornament of a family they didn't recognize.
5. c) They would meet and exchange one special ornament every Christmas.

The Lost Reindeer

Snowville was a small, **charming** town. The **rooftops** were covered in snow, and children laughed and played games every day. Everyone was getting ready for their favorite time of year—Christmas. The streets had many twinkling lights and people could smell fresh gingerbread in the air. Snowville took pride in being known as the 'Christmas Capital' of Canada, and every corner of the town shimmered with holiday spirit.

At the heart of Snowville lived Mia, a 10-year-old with a heart full of **curiosity** and wonder. Her bright blue eyes always seemed to sparkle, especially around Christmas time. Mia loved everything about this season: the

songs, the stories, and most of all, the magic. She lived in a small, cozy house at the end of town. There was a thick forest covered with snow next to her house. The forest was said to be **enchanted,** and Mia would often daydream about the mysteries it held.

One day, while playing outside, making a snowman in her backyard that bordered the woods, Mia saw a **silhouette** in the distance. As the figure neared, her eyes widened in surprise. It was a reindeer, looking lost and scared.

"Mia! Come inside! It's getting cold!" her mom called from the front door.

"But Mom, look! A reindeer!" Mia shouted back, pointing excitedly.

Her mom rolled her eyes, **dismissing** it as her daughter's vivid imagination. "It's probably just a deer, Mia. Come on now."

But Mia's brother, Luke, believed her. He dashed outside, eyes wide with wonder.

"Whoa! Is that one of Santa's reindeers?" he asked in **awe**.

Mia approached the reindeer **cautiously**. "Hey there, are you lost?" The reindeer **nuzzled** her hand as if in reply. Around its neck was a **collar** with a name: "Blitz."

"Blitz? Like... Blitzen?" Luke **whispered**.

Both children knew they needed to help this lost reindeer. "We should take him to Santa!" said Luke.

"But the North Pole is so far away," Mia replied, her voice full of worry.

There was a beautiful small house with a red door between Mia's house and the forest. Smoke came out from its chimney. It belonged to Mr. Jenkins, an elderly man who had lived in Snowville for as long as anyone could remember. He was known for his vast collection of Christmas stories and legends, passed down from generation to generation.

With snowy white hair, a long, wispy beard, and always wearing his signature green sweater, Mr. Jenkins was the **embodiment** of the holiday spirit in Snowville.

Just as Mia and Luke were wondering what to do with Blitz, Mr. Jenkins came out of his house and shuffled over, leaning on his cane. "Well now, what do we have here?" he asked with a twinkle in his eye.

"A lost reindeer, Mr. Jenkins! We think it's Santa's," Mia said.

Mr. Jenkins **chuckled**, "Ah, Blitzen! I've heard stories about him. Let's get him back home."

"But how?" Luke questioned.

Mr. Jenkins leaned in, whispering, "I know a **shortcut**."

The children were curious. They'd heard tales about Mr. Jenkins' adventures, but most people in the neighborhood considered them just gossip.

Following Mr. Jenkins, they ventured into the woods, Blitz trotting alongside. They reached a clearing with a giant, **ornate** door standing alone. "This, kids, is a magical door," he explained.

Mia looked skeptical. "A door in the middle of the woods?"

Mr. Jenkins winked. "Not just any door. It leads directly to the North Pole."

Mia eagerly approached the door and pulled at its large handle. To her surprise, the door wouldn't **budge**. She tried again, pushing, pulling, but nothing.

Mr. Jenkins frowned, confusion on his face. "That's **peculiar**. It's never been stuck before."

Luke looked around and saw a large stone nearby. On it was an **inscription**: "To open the door, the true spirit of Christmas you must show."

Mia and Luke exchanged glances. "What does that mean?"

Mr. Jenkins thought for a moment. "Ah! It means that to open this door, we must **demonstrate** the true meaning of Christmas."

Blitzen, perhaps sensing their confusion, nuzzled Luke's pocket.

Rummaging in his pocket, Luke pulled out the last of his beloved Christmas cookies – a treat he never shared with anyone. He **hesitated** for a moment, then offered it to Blitzen, who ate it happily. As the reindeer crunched on the cookie, the door creaked and slowly swung open, revealing the bustling, colorful workshop of the North Pole on the other side.

"**Selfless** acts of kindness," Mr. Jenkins whispered. "That's the true spirit of Christmas."

"Wow," Luke whispered, his eyes shining bright.

As they walked, elves waved and shouted, "Blitzen! You're back!"

Suddenly, a familiar "Ho, ho, ho!" **echoed**. Santa himself approached, his face a mixture of **relief** and joy. "Blitzen! Where have you been?"

"We found him in Snowville," Mia explained.

Santa chuckled, "Always the adventurer, that one." He turned to the kids. "Thank you, Mia and Luke. Christmas couldn't happen without all of my reindeer."

Luke's face **lit up**. "Does that mean we saved Christmas?"

Santa laughed, "Indeed, you did!" As they prepared to leave, Santa handed them a small bell each. "Ring this if you ever need some Christmas magic," he said with a wink.

Returning home, they realized no time had passed. Their adventure had felt hours long, but it was still the same snowy afternoon in Snowville.

"Mia, Luke, hot cocoa's ready!" their mom called. The siblings exchanged a knowing smile, holding their magical bells close.

New words

- **charming *(adj.)*:** pleasant or delightful.
- **rooftop *(noun)*:** the outside top covering of a building.
- **curiosity *(noun)*:** a strong desire to know or learn something.
- **enchanted *(adj.)*:** filled with wonder or delight.
- **silhouette *(noun)*:** the dark shape or outline of someone or something.
- **dismiss *(verb)*:** to consider something to be unworthy of consideration or irrelevant.
- **awe *(noun)*:** a feeling of great respect, sometimes mixed with fear or surprise.
- **cautiously *(adverb)*:** in a way that is careful to avoid potential problems or dangers.

- **nuzzle** *(verb)*: to rub or push gently against someone or something with the nose or head, often to show affection or comfort.
- **collar** *(noun)*: a band that fits around the neck of an animal, often with a bell or a tag attached.
- **embodiment** *(noun)*: a tangible or visible representation of something abstract.
- **chuckle** *(verb)*: to laugh quietly.
- **whisper** *(verb)*: to speak very softly or quietly.
- **shortcut** *(noun)*: a shorter, more direct route or method than the usual one, often used to save time or effort.
- **ornate** *(adj.)*: made with intricate shapes or decorated with complex patterns.
- **budge** *(verb)*: to move slightly or change position.
- **peculiar** *(adj.)*: strange or odd; unusual.
- **inscription** *(noun)*: words inscribed, as on a monument or in a book.

- **demonstrate** *(verb)*: to show or make clear by using examples or evidence.
- **selfless** *(adj.)*: putting other people's needs and wishes before one's own.
- **echo** *(verb)*: to repeat a sound because the sound waves reflect off a surface.
- **relief** *(noun)*: a feeling of reassurance and relaxation following the release of anxiety or distress.
- **light up** *(verb)*: to become bright or brighter.

Test yourself

1. What is Snowville especially known for during the Christmas season?
 a) Having the biggest Christmas tree.
 b) Being the 'Christmas Capital'.
 c) Having the loudest Christmas carols.

2. What did Mia see in the forest when she was making a snowman?
 a) A lost elf.
 b) Santa Claus.
 c) A scared and lost reindeer.

3. What was written on the reindeer's collar?
 a) Rudolph.
 b) Dasher.
 c) Blitz.

4. Why couldn't Mia initially open the magical gateway in the woods?
    a) She didn't have the key.
    b) She wasn't strong enough.
    c) The door required a demonstration of the true spirit of Christmas.

5. What did Santa give Mia and Luke before they left the North Pole?
    a) A new reindeer.
    b) A magical bell.
    c) A sack of toys.

Discussion

1. What would you do if you found a lost reindeer in your backyard like Mia and Luke did?

2. The door in the woods only opens when someone shows the "true spirit of Christmas." What does the true spirit of Christmas mean to you?

3. What do you think will happen when Mia and Luke use the bell that Santa gave them? Use your imagination!

ANSWERS

1. b) Being the 'Christmas Capital'.
2. c) A scared and lost reindeer.
3. c) Blitz.
4. c) The door required a demonstration of the true spirit of Christmas.
5. b) A magical bell.

Christmas at the Lighthouse

Boston was full of Christmas cheer. There were bright lights, pretty window displays, and people singing carols. But amid all this excitement, young Abigail often dreamt of the sea. With her bright blue eyes and curly brown hair, she loved reading stories about **pirates** and drawing pictures of boats. She even had a small collection of seashells she would pick up during their rare trips to the beach.

Her father, Mr. Longman, was tall with a friendly face and a beard. He was a **marine biologist** and often went on long **expeditions**.

Abigail loved his stories about the sea and its creatures, but she would miss him deeply when he was away. Sometimes, he would be gone for months, and the family couldn't join him on these trips.

At dinner one evening, the Longmans sat around their dining table, the **aroma** of a freshly cooked meal in the air. Mr. Longman, looking up from his plate with a twinkle in his eyes, announced, "I have some exciting news. We're going to spend Christmas at a lighthouse this year."

Abigail, her fork mid-air, looked at him in surprise. "A lighthouse? But Dad, it's Christmas!"

Mrs. Longman, while passing the salad bowl, added, "It's one of your dad's special projects, Abby. He thought we could all use a change of scenery this year."

Lucas, Abigail's younger brother, with his usual excited energy, jumped in, "Like the North Pole? Will there be elves?"

Mr. Longman chuckled, "No, Lucas. It's a lighthouse by the sea. But who knows? Maybe we'll make our own Christmas magic there."

Abigail paused, considering the **proposal**. She always missed her father when he was away on his marine biology trips. "Will you tell us your sea stories every night, Dad?"

Mr. Longman smiled, "Every night. And maybe we'll even make some new stories together."

Lucas's eyes lit up, and even Abigail felt a warm feeling growing inside her. Maybe, just maybe, this Christmas could be an adventure like no other.

When the day came, the family packed their bags. Abigail looked out of her window at the busy city. She thought about the lighthouse. Would it be quiet? Would she miss the city lights and songs?

When they got to the lighthouse, it stood tall by the big blue sea. The sound of the waves was loud, and birds flew in the sky. Abigail felt a bit worried. But soon, she started to like the place.

While Abigail was exploring the rocky shores one morning, she spotted something unusual. Half-buried in the sand, washed up by the recent high tide, was an old wooden chest.

"Lucas!" Abigail called out, her voice filled with excitement. "Come over here! Look what I found!"

Lucas, who was collecting seashells nearby, hurried over. "What is it, Abby?" he asked, his eyes widening at the sight of the chest.

"It looks like a **treasure chest!**" Abigail exclaimed, her imagination running wild.

Lucas bent down, brushing the sand off the top. "Do you think there's gold inside?"

"I don't know," she replied with a grin, "but let's find out!" Together, they managed to pull the chest onto drier land.

Curiosity piqued, they **pried** it open to reveal a collection of old letters, journals, and even some hand-drawn maps.

The letters were from sailors and **lighthouse keepers** who had once celebrated Christmas at this very location. They wrote about their **longing** for home, their makeshift celebrations, and the warmth of **comradeship** that made those cold winter nights bearable.

As they **sifted** through the letters, one in particular caught Abigail's eye. It was written in a delicate handwriting, the ink slightly faded but the words still legible. It read:

December 24th, 1878

My Dearest Eleanor,
As I sit here in the lighthouse, I find peace in the glow of the lantern above. Christmas Eve feels different this year. We may not have the lavish feasts or the grand celebrations, but we have our own little traditions.

Jones, one of the sailors, played his old accordion, and we all sang along. Even old captain Longman, with his rough exterior, couldn't help but hum a few tunes. We had a modest feast: some preserved fruits, freshly baked bread, and a stew that cook managed to make. We even made a small christmas tree from driftwood and adorned it with seashells and bits of colored glass found on the shore.

But the highlight was the gift exchange. We drew names from a hat earlier in the month, and I received a hand-carved wooden trinket from Sam. It's a small ship, a testament to our life at sea. I shall cherish it always.

I miss home terribly, but tonight, amidst the laughter and song, I felt a sense of belonging. It's a reminder that Christmas isn't about where you are, but who you're with.

Warmly,

Thomas.

After reading it out loud, Abigail looked up, her eyes glistening. "This is the celebration we should recreate. It's simple but filled with so much warmth and love."

Her family nodded in agreement, touched by the **sentiment** behind Thomas's words.

"Let's do it," said her mother, wiping away a tear. "Let's make this Christmas one for the books."

The next day, as Christmas morning dawned, the unmistakable aroma of fresh bread filled the lighthouse. Abigail's mother had risen early to bake, as the sailors had detailed in their letters. "Lucas, can you fetch some butter from the fridge?" she asked.

Lucas, with a cheeky grin and dough on his hands, responded, "Only if I get the first slice!"

Abigail, after her beach expedition, exclaimed, "Look at these seashells and colored glass I found! Just like Thomas wrote about!" With her mother's guidance, they started decorating a **driftwood** Christmas tree.

"It's beautiful, Abby," her mother said, admiring their work. "It feels like we've brought a piece of the past to our celebration."

Mr. Longman, **chiseling** away at his driftwood creations, looked up with a twinkle in his eye. "Guess what this is?" he asked, holding up a partially carved figure.

Abigail squinted, then guessed, "A whale? It looks just like the ones you've told us about from your expeditions!"

"You got it!" Mr. Longman chuckled, pleased. "And this one's for you."

As the aroma of stew filled the room, Lucas held up a small **harmonica**. "It's not an **accordion**, but it's the best I could do," he said sheepishly.

Abigail laughed, "It's perfect, Lucas! Let's hear it."

He hesitated for a moment before starting to play a familiar Christmas tune. Soon, the whole family joined in, singing and laughing.

As they exchanged gifts later in the evening, Abigail's mother handed her a delicately wrapped package. "This is special, Abby. Made with love," she said. Inside was a hand-**knitted** scarf in shades of blue that **mirrored** the sea.

"Thank you, mom," Abigail whispered, her eyes **moist** with gratitude.

The rest of the evening was filled with laughter and stories, creating memories that would stay with them for years to come.

As they looked out across the Atlantic, Abigail whispered, "I think this has been one of our best Christmases ever." Her dad wrapped an arm around her, "It's all about making memories, Abby. No matter where we are."

That year, away from the city's noise, the Longman family realized the depth of their bond and the importance of creating new memories. The lighthouse, which Abigail once saw as a lonely place, transformed into a symbol of togetherness and the **enduring** spirit of Christmas.

New words

- **pirate** *(noun)*: a person who robs or attacks ships at sea, often known for their adventurous and lawless behavior.
- **marine biologist** *(noun)*: a scientist who studies organisms in the ocean or other marine bodies of water.
- **expedition** *(noun)*: a journey or voyage made for a special purpose, like research.
- **lighthouse** *(noun)*: a tower or building containing a light to warn or guide ships at sea.
- **twinkle** *(verb)*: to shine with a light that blinks or gleams intermittently.
- **aroma** *(noun)*: a pleasant and distinctive smell.
- **proposal** *(noun)*: a suggestion or plan put forward for consideration.
- **treasure chest** *(noun)*: a box or container holding valuable items, often associated with pirates or hidden riches.

- **lighthouse keeper *(noun)*:** a person responsible for maintaining and operating a lighthouse.
- **longing *(noun)*:** a strong desire or wish for something or to do something.
- **makeshift *(adj.)*:** made to be used for a short time only when nothing better is available.
- **one for the books *(phrase)*:** something noteworthy, remarkable, or memorable.
- **glisten *(verb)*:** to shine with a shimmering or sparkling light.
- **driftwood *(noun)*:** wood that has been washed onto a shore or beach by the action of winds, tides, or waves.
- **comradeship *(noun)*:** friendship and shared experiences among a group.
- **sift *(verb)*:** to examine or sort through carefully.
- **accordion *(noun)*:** a musical instrument with folding bellows and keyboard.
- **trinket *(noun)*:** a small ornament or item of jewelry that is of little value.

- **cherish** *(verb)*: to hold or treat as dear; to feel love for.
- **pry** *(verb)*: to use force to open or remove something.
- **moist** *(adj.)*: a little wet; damp.
- **solace** *(noun)*: comfort or relief in a time of distress.
- **sentiment** *(noun)*: a feeling or emotion.
- **knit** *(verb)*: to make (a garment, fabric, etc.) by interlocking loops of yarn by means of needles or by machine.
- **mirrored** *(verb)*: to reflect in or as if in a mirror.
- **chisel** *(verb)*: to carve or cut into a material using a chisel.
- **harmonica** *(noun)*: a small wind instrument played by blowing and drawing air through reed-filled holes.
- **hesitate** *(verb)*: to be reluctant or to wait to act because of fear, uncertainty, or indecision.
- **enduring** *(adj.)*: lasting; persistent.

Test yourself

1. Why did Abigail feel a mix of emotions about spending Christmas at the lighthouse?

    a) She didn't like the sea.

    b) She was afraid of lighthouses.

    c) She was excited about the adventure.

    d) She would miss the city's festive cheer.

2. What did Abigail and Lucas find on the beach?

    a) A treasure map.

    b) A message in a bottle.

    c) An old wooden chest.

    d) A sailor's hat.

3. What did the chest contain?
    a) Gold and jewelry.
    b) Old letters and hand-drawn maps.
    c) Pirate clothes.
    d) Marine tools.

4. What was the highlight of the sailor's Christmas celebration as mentioned in Thomas's letter?
    a) A grand feast.
    b) Fireworks.
    c) Gift exchange.
    d) Singing carols by the fire.

5. What instrument did Lucas play on Christmas day?
    a) A guitar.
    b) A drum.
    c) An accordion.
    d) A harmonica.

1. Would you prefer to spend Christmas by
    the sea or in a city? Why?

2. What do you think is the main message
    or lesson of the story? Explain.

3. If you could spend Christmas in an
    unusual or different place, where would it
    be and why?

ANSWERS

1. d) She would miss the city's festive cheer.
2. c) An old wooden chest.
3. b) Old letters and hand-drawn maps.
4. c) Gift exchange.
5. d) A harmonica.

The Magical Snow Globe

In the small village of Frostwick, England, where the streets were covered with snow and chimneys sent out warm smoke, everyone was preparing for Christmas.

Sarah, a girl with bright green eyes, lived in a lovely red-brick house near the village center. She loved wearing her knitted scarf, a special gift from her grandmother. Her younger brother, Toby, was always with her, looking for new adventures.

One cold December afternoon, Sarah and Toby were **rummaging** through the **attic**.

Among the dusty boxes and cobwebs, they found memories of many past Christmases. Sarah opened a box revealing old, worn-out Christmas decorations. Toby pulled out a faded green and red stocking with his name beautifully **embroidered** on it.

"Remember this, Sarah? Mum used to fill it with candies every Christmas," he said, a hint of **nostalgia** in his voice.

In another corner, Sarah uncovered a stack of **vinyl** records. "Oh, these are Granny's old Christmas albums!" she exclaimed, holding one up to look at its cover. It showed a snowy village scene, much like Frostwick. Toby excitedly looked through them, finding familiar holiday tunes that their family would play every year.

While Sarah was **reminiscing** about Christmases past, listening to the faint echo of songs in her head, Toby stumbled upon another box. "Look at this!" He held up a beautiful **snow globe** with a tiny **replica** of Frostwick inside.

Sarah looked closely. "This is our village! But there's something special about this snow globe."

As she looked into the globe, the tiny lights in the miniature houses began to flicker gently, and a soft, **enchanting** melody played. The tiny snowflakes formed beautiful patterns. The miniature Frostwick seemed alive, with trees swaying and tiny people waving at them.

Sarah was really excited. "Toby! Come and see!" she called, holding the snow globe carefully in her hands. She showed it to him, hoping the lights would start to twinkle and the beautiful song would play again. But nothing happened. The snow inside just sat there, and the tiny village looked normal.

Toby looked at her and smiled. "It's just a snow globe, Sarah. It's pretty, but I don't see anything special." Sarah felt sad. She knew what she had seen, but now it seemed like just her imagination.

Sarah sighed, feeling a mix of disappointment and confusion. She placed the snow globe back into the box, but she couldn't shake off the feeling that there was more to it than met the eye.

Over the next few days, Sarah would often sneak up to the attic, just to have another look. Every time, she hoped the snow globe would reveal its magic again. And every time, nothing happened. Toby noticed her frequent visits and teased, "Still trying to make the little village dance?"

Sarah just nodded, "I know what I saw, Toby. I just don't understand why it won't happen again."

One evening, as Christmas approached, Sarah decided to show the snow globe to Toby once more, hoping the magic would reveal itself. They sat together in the attic.

Sarah took a deep breath, held the snow globe close to her heart, and whispered a Christmas wish. To both their **astonishments**, the room began to spin. Snowflakes swirled around them, and the world blurred.

When they opened their eyes, they were no longer in their attic but standing in the middle of the miniature Frostwick from the snow globe. The buildings **loomed** above them, the soft melody surrounded them, and the snow under their feet felt real.

"Sarah... where are we?" Toby exclaimed, looking around in awe.

"We're inside the snow globe!" Sarah whispered, her eyes wide with wonder. They saw the tiny figures from before, who now appeared life-sized, waving and welcoming them.

A group of villagers approached. "Ah, you've made it! We've been waiting for you," a jolly man said, extending a hand. "I'm Mayor Snowton. Every year, we invite someone with a true Christmas spirit to celebrate with us."

Sarah and Toby were treated to a grand feast, participated in village games, and danced under the twinkling lights. As the evening deepened, the village seemed to offer new wonders.

"Would you like a **bird's-eye view** of Frostwick?" asked a villager named Finn, pointing to a sleigh attached to a group of floating balloons.

Before they knew it, Sarah and Toby were soaring above the village in the balloon-sleigh. From this **vantage point**, they could see their actual village outside the snow globe. Every house was **adorned** with fairy lights, making it look like a starry sky on a clear night. However, one house stood out from the rest. It was dimly lit and looked rather lonely amidst the festive atmosphere.

"That's Mrs. Winterton's house," whispered Sarah. Mrs. Winterton was an elderly lady who lived by herself, two doors down from Sarah and Toby. They knew her, but they had never realised how isolated she seemed during the holidays.

As they continued to float, they saw scenes inside the houses too. At Mrs. Winterton's, they saw her sitting by a fireplace with a solitary candle, looking out of the window with a **forlorn** expression.

The balloon-sleigh ride was **exhilarating**, but that sight left a lasting impact on the siblings. They felt a new sense of purpose, understanding the importance of community and looking out for one another.

After their return, as midnight approached, Mayor Snowton said, "It's time for you to return. Remember what you've seen and learned. Let the spirit of Christmas guide your way."

Once Sarah and Toby were back in their attic, the wonder of their adventure inside the snow globe still fresh in their minds, they couldn't help but think about Mrs. Winterton.

"We need to do something," Sarah whispered.

Toby nodded. "Let's make her feel special this Christmas."

The siblings quickly put together a basket of goodies: freshly baked cookies, a warm knitted scarf, and a small potted plant. They also included a handwritten note, inviting her over for Christmas dinner.

Bundling up against the cold, they made their way to Mrs. Winterton's house. As they approached, they could see the dim light from her window. They knocked softly, and after a moment, the door creaked open to reveal Mrs. Winterton's surprised face.

"Sarah, Toby! What brings you here at this hour?" she asked with a hint of a smile.

"We just wanted to spread a little Christmas cheer," Sarah replied, handing her the basket.

Mrs. Winterton's eyes **moistened** as she looked at the basket and then at the two children. "Oh, you sweethearts," she said, pulling them towards her for a gentle huge.

The evening turned into a delightful one as they shared stories and laughter over cups of hot cocoa. Mrs. Winterton had so many tales from past Christmases, and the children listened with **rapt** attention.

As they left her house, the night sky above was filled with stars, but the warmth they felt inside was brighter than any starlight. They had not only experienced magic that day but also discovered the joy of bringing a little light to someone else's world.

From that year on, Mrs. Winterton joined the siblings and their family for Christmas dinner. It became a **cherished** tradition, reminding them that even the simplest **gestures** can create lasting memories and bonds that strengthen over time. The true magic of Christmas, they realized, was not just in wondrous adventures but in the heartfelt moments shared with loved ones.

New words

- **snow globe** *(noun)*: a clear spherical ornament containing a scene or figure, with water and often glitter, that, when shaken, looks like falling snow.
- **rummage** *(verb)*: to search for something by moving things around, typically in a hurried or messy manner.
- **attic** *(noun)*: a space or room just below the roof of a building, often used for storing things.
- **embroider** *(verb)*: to decorate fabric by sewing patterns on it with thread.
- **nostalgia** *(noun)*: a sentimental longing or wistful affection for a period in the past.
- **vinyl** *(noun)*: a type of plastic that records are made of; used here to refer to record albums.
- **replica** *(noun)*: a copy or reproduction of a work of art.

- **reminisce** *(verb)*: recalling past events or experiences, often with a sense of nostalgia or fondness.
- **enchanting** *(adj.)*: delightfully charming or attractive.
- **astonishment** *(noun)*: a great surprise or amazement.
- **loom** *(verb)*: to appear as a large, often frightening or unclear shape or object.
- **bird's-eye view** *(noun)*: a view from above, as if seen by a bird in flight.
- **exhilarating** *(adj.)*: making one feel very happy, animated, or elated.
- **vantage point** *(noun)*: a position that allows a clear, broad view or understanding of something.
- **adorn** *(verb)*: to decorate or add beauty to.
- **forlorn** *(adjective)*: looking or feeling sad or abandoned.
- **cherish** *(verb)*: to hold dear; feel or show affection for.
- **gesture** *(noun)*: An act or action done to show goodwill, kindness, or appreciation.

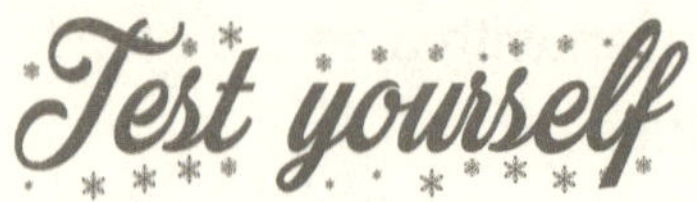

1. Where did Sarah and Toby find the magical snow globe?

    a) In the garden

    b) At the village center

    c) In the attic

    d) In the basement

2. Who is Mayor Snowton?

    a) The mayor of the real Frostwick village.

    b) The jolly man inside the snow globe.

    c) The siblings' grandfather.

3. What did Sarah and Toby see when they soared above the village in the balloon-sleigh?

      a) The entire world.

      b) Their own village.

      c) A snowy forest.

4. What did Mrs. Winterton and the children do on the night they visited her?

      a) They sang carols.

      b) They exchanged gifts.

      c) They listened to old Christmas music.

      d) They shared stories and drank hot cocoa.

5. What became a cherished tradition after the adventure?

      a) Visiting the snow globe every year.

      b) Listening to old Christmas albums.

      c) Mrs. Winterton joining the siblings and their family for Christmas dinner.

1. Have you ever felt close to your community or helped someone during the holidays?

2. Why should we think of lonely people during holidays? How can we include everyone?

3. What does the "true magic of Christmas" mean to you?

1. c) In the attic
2. b) The jolly man inside the snow globe.
3. b) Their own village.
4. d) They shared stories and drank hot cocoa.
5. c) Mrs. Winterton joining the siblings and their family for Christmas dinner.

Molly's Enchanted Christmas Scarf

Molly, a young woman with beautiful long brown hair and an infectious smile was exploring the streets of the city where she lived. Looking up, she could see the skyscrapers covered with sparkling lights. Although it was below 0 outside, she loved her city during Christmas time. Everyone seemed to have a smile on their face. Today, Molly was **on a mission**: to find the perfect Christmas gift for her mother.

Molly and her mother shared a bond unlike any other. Christmas was their special time, a tradition they had cherished since Molly was a child. They would bake cookies, decorate the house, and sing carols. But this year was different. Molly's mother had faced health challenges, making the festive season a quiet affair. Molly wanted to reignite the spark and joy of Christmas for her mother, making this gift even more significant.

She spent hours looking in all the different stores, but nothing seemed quite right. Her mother was very important to her, so she knew she needed something extra special. As she was about **to give up**, she found a cute little shop, hidden from the main street. A sign above the door read, "Mrs. Winters' Wonders." Curious, Molly decided to enter.

The shop was a **labyrinth** of shelves filled with curious objects. Each corner seemed to hold its own little world – snow globes with mini winter wonderlands, intricate wooden toys that moved with clockwork precision,

and candles that released the sweetest scents when lit. The walls, lined with deep green wallpaper, had small golden bells that jingled at intervals, adding to the shop's magical ambiance.

An **elderly** lady with silver hair stood behind the counter, smiling kindly.

"Hello, dear. Welcome to my shop," she greeted.

"Thank you," Molly replied, glancing around. "You have such a **charming** place here."

"Why, thank you! We try to keep the spirit of Christmas alive throughout the year. Anything in particular you're searching for?"

Molly hesitated for a moment. "I'm looking for a special gift for my mother. I've been to so many shops today, but nothing seemed right."

"Well, take your time and look around. Sometimes the perfect gift just appears when you least expect it," the elderly lady said **with a wink**.

Molly smiled and began to **browse**. As she did, a particular scarf caught her attention. Blue and silver in color, it **shimmered** softly under the lights. "This is beautiful," she said, picking it up to admire it closer.

The old lady nodded. "That is the Enchanted Christmas Scarf. It has special magic."

Molly looked surprised. "Magic?"

"Yes," replied the lady. "When you wear it, you'll feel the true spirit of Christmas. But remember, it's not just about the scarf. It's about the love and joy you share."

Excited, Molly decided to buy the scarf. She couldn't wait to experience its magic. **Little did she know**, this scarf would make her Christmas unforgettable.

After buying the scarf, Molly went straight home. She carefully wrapped it in shiny paper and placed it under the Christmas tree. Every night, she noticed tiny shimmers of light peeking from beneath the **wrapping paper.** It felt as though the scarf held some mysterious magic.

Every night, as Molly watched the subtle glimmers from the scarf, her anticipation grew. She often found herself lost in thoughts, wondering what kind of magic it held. Would it dazzle with lights? Or perhaps play a song? The wait felt like forever, and every day she had to resist the urge to open the scarf.

Christmas morning finally arrived. Everyone gathered around the tree and opened their presents, but Molly was especially **eager** to see her mother's reaction to her gift. As her mom unwrapped Molly's present, the shimmering light seemed to grow brighter.

"Oh, Molly," her mother **gasped**, looking at the shimmering blue and silver scarf. "It's **stunning**." She wrapped it around her neck and as she did, a soft, calming wind began to circulate the room. The wind seemed to whisper sweet words and memories.

Molly's dad, who had been **distant** lately due to stresses at work, suddenly looked relaxed. The **weight on his shoulders** seemed to lift. "Do you remember our first Christmas together?" he asked Molly's mother, smiling.

She nodded, tears forming in her eyes. "Yes, the year when everything went wrong but felt so right because we had each other."

He continued, "And how about the year when we tried to cook dinner, but the oven broke, and we ended up eating sandwiches by candlelight?"

She laughed. "Oh, I'll never forget that! The kitchen was a mess, but we danced in the living room with sandwiches in our hands. It was imperfect but so memorable."

Molly watched, surprised and warmed. Over the past few months, her parents had been so busy they barely spent time together, and small disagreements had started to grow. But now, it was as if they were reliving their happiest memories, brought back by the magic of the scarf.

Seeing her parents reconnect like this, Molly felt a warmth in her heart. She realized that the scarf wasn't just a physical gift; it carried the power to remind people of their happiest moments and the importance of **cherishing** love.

As the evening went on, the house filled with laughter and stories from the past. Molly's mother looked stronger and happier. The tiredness and sickness seemed to go away. This brought tears to Molly's eyes—she had never seen her parents so healthy and happy. The night seemed to last forever, allowing them more time to enjoy each other's company.

When it was finally time to head to bed, Molly's mother draped the scarf around her shoulders, smiling at Molly. "Thank you," she whispered, her eyes shining with gratitude.

Molly nodded, squeezing her mother's hand. "Merry Christmas, Mom."

"Merry Christmas, sweetheart," her mother replied.

And as the lights **dimmed**, the magic of the scarf continued to glow, reminding them all that the best gifts are not the ones you can touch but the memories you create and the love you share.

New words

- **on a mission *(phrase)*:** determined to get something done.
- **labyrinth *(noun)*:** a maze or a complex system of paths or tunnels in which it is easy to get lost.
- **elderly *(adj.)*:** being old or aging.
- **charming *(adj.)*:** pleasant and attractive.
- **browse *(verb)*:** to look around casually, without a specific purpose.

- **little did she know *(phrase)*:** used to indicate that someone is unaware of something that will happen.
- **shimmer *(verb)*:** to shine with a flickering or wavering light.
- **wrapping paper *(noun)*:** decorative paper for covering and beautifying presents.
- **eager *(adj.)*:** wanting to do or have something very much.
- **gasp *(verb)*:** to take a sudden, short intake of breath as a result of surprise.
- **stunning *(adj.)*:** extremely impressive or attractive.
- **whisper *(verb)*:** to speak very softly.
- **distant *(adj.)*:** detached, not engaged or involved.
- **weight on his shoulders *(idiom)*:** a heavy burden or responsibility.
- **cherishing *(verb)*:** treating with care and affection; holding dear.

- **gratitude** *(noun)*: thankfulness and appreciation.
- **dim** *(verb)*: make or become less bright or distinct.
- **on a mission** *(phrase)*: determined to get something done.
- **give up** *(phrasal verb)*: to stop trying.
- **with a wink** *(phrase)*: to close one eye quickly as a signal.

Test yourself

1. What is Molly's mission during her walk in the city?

    a) To see the Christmas lights.
    b) To buy a gift for her friend.
    c) To buy a gift for her mother.

2. What did Molly buy from "Mrs. Winters' Wonders"?

    a) A dress.
    b) A necklace.
    c) A scarf.

3. Why had Molly's dad been distant lately?

    a) He was busy with work.
    b) He was on vacation.
    c) He didn't like Christmas.

4. What happened when Molly's mother wrapped the scarf around her neck?

       a) It became very cold.

       b) The lights turned off.

       c) A soft, calming wind began to circulate.

5. What did Molly and her parents do during Christmas evening?

       a) They went out for dinner.

       b) They shared stories and memories.

       c) They watched a movie.

Discussion

1. Have you ever gotten or given a meaningful gift?

2. Do you think memories with loved ones are better gifts than physical items?

3. How can traditions and memories make families stronger?

4. What's the funniest Christmas gift you've ever received or given?

ANSWERS

1. c) To buy a gift for her mother.
2. c) A scarf.
3. a) He was busy with work.
4. c) A soft, calming wind began to circulate.
5. b) They shared stories and memories.

The Christmas Train

In the heart of a snowy town, teenagers gathered at a local café, sipping hot cocoa and laughing about their day. Among them was Charlie, a tall 16-year-old with messy brown hair and a **rebellious glint** in his eyes. A few tables away, festive decorations lit up the space, and Christmas music played softly in the background.

Lucas, one of Charlie's friends, said excitedly, "My little sister said she heard Santa's reindeer on our roof last year. She's certain!"

Charlie laughed, "Lucas, you don't believe her, do you?"

Lucas grinned, "I don't know. There's definitely something magical about this time of year. Why not believe?"

"Santa Claus? Seriously?" Charlie remarked, **rolling his eyes**. "I mean, we're not kids anymore."

Jenna, a close friend of Charlie's, looked at him playfully. "Oh, come on, Charlie! You used to be **obsessed** with Christmas."

Charlie **shrugged**, "That was ages ago."

She challenged him, "Charlie, just because we're teens doesn't mean we can't enjoy the magic of Christmas."

Across the table, Mia chimed in, "Jenna's right. The holidays are about more than just Santa. It's about the spirit, the giving, and the love."

As the evening wore on, Charlie became **lost in thought**. He glanced outside the café window, watching the snowflakes gently fall, painting the town white. Just as he was about to turn back to his friends, a sudden, bright light appeared in the distance, growing larger and nearer. The ground slightly **trembled** and a faint but increasing sound reached Charlie's ears — chug, chug, chug.

"What's that noise?" Lucas asked, his gaze following Charlie's.

Before anyone could answer, the café was filled with the echoing sound of a train whistle, startling everyone inside. The light grew so bright that for a moment, the whole café seemed to glow.

"What on earth...?" Jenna began, but the light and sound faded as swiftly as they appeared.

Charlie tried to **brush it off**. "Probably just some festival thing," he mumbled, though he couldn't ignore the uneasy feeling it gave him.

That night, as Charlie **snuggled** into bed, he couldn't shake off the **eerie** incident from earlier. The conversations of the evening mixed with the train's sound echoed in his mind. Suddenly, another loud whistle sounded, and the world around him moved. He felt a jolt, and when he blinked his eyes open, he found himself no longer in his cozy bedroom but on the soft seat of a **vintage** train.

The carriage was filled with **youngsters** whispering, their eyes wide with a mix of fear and excitement. Next to him, a teen boy with a baseball cap extended his hand, "Max," he introduced himself. "Got any idea what's going on?"

Charlie shook his head, equally **baffled**. "None. But we need to figure it out."

Deciding to explore, they moved to the next carriage. The room was **draped** in **velvety** red and gold fabric. A projector flashed incomplete Christmas carol lyrics onto a screen, while a small crowd of teenagers tried filling in the missing words.

Max chuckled, "I haven't sung these since I was a kid!"

A line of the carol played: "Jingle bells, jingle bells, jingle all the...?"

Charlie found himself singing along, "Way! Oh what fun it is to ride in a one-horse open sleigh."

Max grinned, "See? It's not all 'kid stuff'. There's magic in these moments."

As the train journey continued, Charlie began to see the truth in Max's words. They explored more carriages, each presenting a new enchanting challenge.

With every challenge, Charlie's **skepticism** melted, replaced by the awe he felt in younger years.The laughter, the singing, the shared experiences; they were all pieces of the magic of Christmas he'd forgotten.

Hours seemed like minutes, and before they knew it, the train stopped. They were greeted by the twinkling lights of the North Pole and the jolly smile of Santa Claus. "Welcome!" Santa exclaimed, his voice deep and warm. "This journey was created for those who've lost touch with the magic of Christmas."

Charlie, looking around at the wonder of the North Pole, felt a **surge** of emotion. "I... I had forgotten. But now I remember," he admitted, his voice soft.

Handing Charlie a small wrapped gift, Santa said, "For you, to remember today and the joy you've rediscovered."

The return journey had an even greater feel of nostalgia. Everyone on the train shared stories, laughed, and sang carols. It was truly magical and Charlie hadn't smiled so much in years.

Upon reaching his hometown, Charlie stepped out of the train, the small wrapped gift in his hand. The café, the conversation, everything seemed like a distant memory, yet the emotions were fresh.

The next day, at the same café, Charlie unwrapped his gift in front of Jenna and his friends — a hand-carved ornament with the North Pole train etched on it. Everyone was amazed by his story of the magical journey.

Jenna smiled warmly at Charlie, "I told you the magic was real."

Lucas chimed in, laughing, "Next time, take me with you!"

Mia agreed, "Yeah! I want to see the North Pole too!"

Charlie grinned, feeling a warmth that wasn't just from the cocoa. "Well, there's always next Christmas. But for now, let's cherish this one."

And so, surrounded by friends and holding onto his gift from Santa, Charlie celebrated the true spirit of Christmas.

New Words

- **in the heart of *(figure of speech)*:** at the center or core of something.
- **rebellious *(adj.)*:** resisting control or authority.
- **glint *(noun)*:** a small, bright flash of light.
- **to roll one's eyes *(idiomatic expression)*:** moving your eyes upwards as a sign of annoyance or boredom.
- **obsessed *(adj.)*:** having or showing excessive or compulsive concern with something.
- **shrug *(verb)*:** raise the shoulders to express indifference or uncertainty.
- **lost in thought *(idiomatic expression)*:** deep in contemplation or thinking so intensely that one is unaware of one's surroundings.
- **tremble *(verb)*:** shake involuntarily, typically due to anxiety or excitement.

- **brush it off** *(idiomatic expression):* Disregard or dismiss something as unimportant.
- **eerie** *(adj.)*: strange and frightening.
- **snuggle** *(verb)*: settled into a warm, comfortable, and protected position.
- **vintage** *(adj.)*: denoting something from the past of high quality.
- **youngsters** *(noun)*: young people, often children or teenagers.
- **baffled** *(adj.)*: confused or perplexed.
- **drape** *(verb)*: covered or decorated with cloth in a flowing or hanging manner.
- **velvety** *(adj.)*: smooth, soft, and thick.
- **skepticism** *(noun)*: a skeptical attitude; doubt regarding the truth or reliability of something.
- **surge** *(noun)*: a sudden powerful forward or upward movement.

Test yourself

1. What were the teenagers doing at the start of the story?
>a) Ice-skating in the park.
>b) Sipping hot cocoa at a café.
>c) Watching a Christmas parade.

2. How did Charlie initially feel about the magic of Christmas?
>a) He believed wholeheartedly.
>b) He was skeptical and thought it was for kids.
>c) He didn't care either way.

3. What strange event happened at the café that caught Charlie's attention?

      a) A surprise visit from Santa Claus.

      b) A bright light and the sound of a train whistle.

      c) The café's lights went out suddenly.

4. Where did Charlie find himself after hearing the train whistle at night in his bedroom?

      a) In a snowy forest.

      b) At the North Pole.

      c) On the soft seat of a vintage train.

5. What gift did Santa give to Charlie?

      a) A hand-carved ornament with the North Pole train etched on it.

      b) A magic reindeer.

      c) A bag of Christmas candies.

Discussion

1. Do you see holidays or special days differently now than you did a few years ago? How?

2. Can you think of a time when something surprised you and made you feel really happy or excited, even if you didn't expect it to?

3. Have you ever had to do something a bit challenging, but it helped you learn or realize something cool about yourself?

4. If you could go on a magic adventure, where would you go and what would you hope to find out or learn?

ANSWERS

1. b) Sipping hot cocoa at a café.
2. b) He was skeptical and thought it was for kids.
3. b) A bright light and the sound of a train whistle.
4. c) On the soft seat of a vintage train.
5. a) A hand-carved ornament with the North Pole train etched on it.

Are you ready to take your English learning journey to the next level? Then join our private Facebook community of fellow learners! It's a friendly and supportive space where you can share, learn, and practice English.

Just scan the QR code and you'll be taken straight to our Facebook page. See you there!

facebook.com/groups/learnenglishhub

Thanks for reading this book. We hope you've had a great time with it and improved your English!

As an author, I'm always eager to hear what you think, so I'd love it if you could take a moment to **leave a review**. Your honest feedback helps me improve my writing and also helps other readers decide if this book is right for them. Plus, I'd just really appreciate it! :)

Visit us at
www.bellanovabooks.com/english
for more great books to continue your learning journey.